M000103980

Instant Pot Keto Recipes Cookbook 2019

**Ketogenic Diet for Beginners' Cookbook.
Quick and Easy High Fat Meals' Guide For Your
Pressure Cooker**

Table of Contents

Introduction..6

Chapter 1 – Beef Recipes 8

  1. Juicy beef...8

  2. Lime Chili Beef Bowl..10

  3. Keto Lasagna..12

  4. Taco Meat 14

  5. Meat Rich Stew..16

  6. Tender Juicy Meatballs...18

  7. Cabbage and Beef..20

  8. Steak Bites...22

Chapter 2 – Breakfast Recipes 24

  1. Pepper Broccoli & Ham Frittata.......................24

  2. Egg Bake with Cheese 26

  3. Frittata with cheese...28

  4. Crustless Meat Quiche..30

  5. Egg Muffins 32

  6. Simple Casserole...34

  7. Asparagus Frittata 36

  8. Egg Cups 38

  9. Breakfast Sandwich...40

  10. Blueberry Muffins..42

Chapter 3 – Fish and Sea Food 44

  1. Tomato Sauce Scallops 44

  2. Simple and tasty Clams 46

  3. Teriyaki Salmon..48

  4. Fish Curry..50

  5. Lemon Salmon 52

  6. Coconut Shrimp...54

  7. Creamy Shrimp..56

Chapter 4 – Vegetable and Bean Dishes 58

  1. Zucchini Noodles..58

  2. Spaghetti Squash..60

  3. Creamed Spinach..62

4. Cabbage Rice..64

5. Mashed Cauliflower 66

6. Brussels Sprouts...68

7. Green Beans...70

Chapter 5 – Soups & Stews...72

1. Spinach Pork Stew...72

2. Pork Stew..74

3. Beef Veggie Soup..76

4. Bacon Chicken Chowder..78

5. Chicken Soup...80

6. Cheeseburger Soup...82

7. Noodle Soup 84

8. Chicken Buffalo Simple Soup...86

9. Chicken Enchilada Simple Soup..88

10. Best and Simple Beef Stew...90

Chapter 6 – Poultry Recipes 92

1. Chicken Meatballs...92

2. Juicy Simple Chicken Breasts...94

3. The Perfect Chicken Wings..96

4. Crack Chicken 98

5. Simplified Delicious Turkey Breast...100

6. Turkey Chili 102

7. Whole Chicken..104

Chapter 7 – Pork Recipes 106

1. Veggies Pork Tenderloin..106

2. Juicy Chops 108

3. Carnitas...110

4. Pork Roast 112

5. Cauliflower Pork Bowl...114

6. Tomato Chili 116

7. Ribs in 30 minutes...118

8. Pulled Pork..120

Chapter 8 – Eggs and Dairy...122

1. Burrito Bowl...122

2. Stuffed Avocado..124

3. Cheddar Bacon Salad..126

4. Spicy Egg Avocado 128

5. Fast and Simple Egg Salad 130

6. Egg Bacon Sour Cream Salad 132

7. Egg Avocado Wonder 134

Chapter 9 – Quick Snacks..136

1. Cauliflower Hummus 136

2. Cauliflower Tots 138

3. Cauliflower rice 140

4. Boiled Egg...142

5. Artichoke Snack 144

6. Steamed Asparagus 146

7. Spiced Nuts...148

10. Keto Desserts 150

1. Cinnamon Apples...150

2. Strawberry Compote 152

3. Lime Curd..154

4. Coconut Custard 156

5. Mug Cakes...158

6. Cheesecake 160

7. Peanut Cheesecake..162

8. Peanut Bites 164

Conclusion...166

Introduction

Do you want to know how to get more benefits from a Keto diet, and know more about home cooking? You can get even more by using an Instant Pot. Keto on its own has health and dietary benefits, but with the instant pot, all those benefits are enhanced, and it makes it a lot easier to cook.

Think about it; now, everyone enjoys standing over the stove and cook different meals in order to reach ketosis. Instant Pot is the best solution for this. Most recipes are just dumped and cooked, while others require just a few minutes sautéing. There is no difficult recipe with the instant pot. All you need to do is get the ingredients you need and follow the steps to prepare it.

I want to remind you about the benefits that we get when we are on a keto diet. Then, together with the instant pot benefits, you will see that you will get one incredible combination.

Keto Benefits:
- Weight loss
- Maintaining weight
- Overall health
- Lowers the risk of diabetes
- Lowers high blood pressure
- Helps with epilepsy
- Triglycerides drop
- Good Cholesterol Increased (HDL)
- Therapeutic for Brain disorders
- And more!!!

Instant Pot Benefits
- Fast Cooking; meals are done in 30 minutes or less
- A machine for several cooking modes
- Tastier and healthier food
- Always tender meat
- Easy and simple to use
- No noise, smell or steam
- Great size options
- Affordable

In the weight-loss and fitness world, the ketogenic diet has become one of the most practiced diets. The main reason is that it lowers our appetite, gives us strength and energy and it optimizes fat - loss. But it is not just that, it also promotes health.

Well, keto is based on food that is high in fat. This means meat, and other fats sources are your options. For this, you need this machine to get the best meat cooked in 30 minutes, keeping it juicy and tender.

So, this means that if you truly want to experience keto in the best way, you need to cook the following recipes using instant pot. Furthermore, the recipes in this book can be easily added in any weekly keto meal plan

Chapter 1 – Beef Recipes

1. Juicy beef

Prep: 10min/**Cook:** 30min/**Total:** 40min
Servings: 6/**Calories:** 800/**Fat:** 70g
Protein: 31g/**Carbs:** 4g

Ingredients:
- 3 lbs. of Beef roast cut into 3 equal pieces
- 1 tbsp. of Olive oil
- 1 jar (1pint) of pepper rings, drained, but ¼ cup reserved
- 2 tbsp. of Seasoning mix, Ranch dressing
- 2 tbsp. of Italian zesty seasoning
- 1 cup of water
- 8 tbsp. of Butter

Directions:

1. Turn on sauté mode. Drizzle 1 tbsp. of olive oil. Once hot, brown the sides of the beef pieces.

2. Stop the sauté mode and pour water. Add reserve juices, pepper rings, seasoning mixes over the meat. Place the butter sticks on top.

3. Close the lid and cook for 30 minutes at high pressure.
4. Once done let the pressure release naturally.
5. Break the meat with salad sheer or forks.
6. Serve with cauliflower rice and enjoy!

2. Lime Chili Beef Bowl

Prep: 8min/**Cook:** 10min/**Total:** 18min
Servings: 4/**Calories:** 570/**Fat:** 36g
Protein: 52g/**Carbs:** 2g

Ingredients:

- 2 lbs. of Steak strips, fajita; cut into small cubes
- 1 tbsp. of Water
- 2 tsp. of fresh Lime juice
- 1 tsp. of Garlic, minced
- 1 tbsp. of Olive oil
- ½ tsp. of Chili Powder
- ½ tsp. of Salt
- ½ tsp. of Black pepper
- 3 diced Avocados

Directions:

1. Turn on sauté. Add the oil.
2. Once heated, add the garlic. Cook for 30 seconds–1 minute.
3. Add all other ingredients. Mix well.

4. Close the lid and cook 10 minutes on High pressure.
5. Quick release the pressure.
6. Turn on sauté. Stir and break the meat into smaller chunks.
7. Stir and cook until the liquid reduces by half.
8. Let it cool and then serve over diced avocado and enjoy!

3. Keto Lasagna

Prep: 10min/**Cook:** 25min /**Total:** 35min
Servings: 8/**Calories:** 365/**Fat:** 25g
Protein: 25g /**Carbs:** 6g

Ingredients:
- 1 lb. of Ground beef
- 1 Onion, small, chopped
- 2 Garlic cloves, minced
- ½ cup of Parmesan Cheese
- 1 ½ cups of Ricotta Cheese
- 1 Egg, large
- 8 oz. of Mozzarella, sliced
- 25 oz. of Marinara sauce
- Olive oil

Directions:

1. Set sauté setting and drizzle some olive oil. Add the onion, garlic and ground beef. Cook until brown.

2. In the meantime, combine the egg, parmesan, and ricotta in a bowl. Mix well.

3. Drain the grease and set aside the meat.

4. In another bowl, add the marinara and add the meat. Stir well. (Keep ½ cup).

5. In a round dish that fits inside the pot, place ½ of the meat mixture, and then add the cheese mixture. Repeat the process. Top with the reserved sauce.

6. Pour 1 cup water in the pot. Place a trivet and place the round dish. Cover the dish loosely with foil.

7. Attach the lid and cook for 9 minutes at high pressure.

8. Quick release the pressure and serve.

4. Taco Meat

Prep: 5min/**Cook:** 10min/**Total:** 15min
Servings: 8/**Calories:** 195/**Fat:** 10g
Protein: 21g/**Carbs:** 4g

Ingredients:
- 2 lbs. of ground Beef
- 1 cup of Tomato sauce, unsalted
- ½ cup of Bell Pepper, diced
- ½ cup of Onion, diced
- 3 tbsp. of Taco Seasoning
- 1 tsp. of Olive oil or avocado oil
- Cilantro, fresh (optional)

Directions:

1. Turn on sauté and add oil. Brown the beef. Turn off function.
2. Add the rest of the ingredients. Stir.
3. Cook on high pressure for 8 minutes.
4. You can either quick release the pressure or let the pressure release naturally.
5. Serve into plates garnished with cilantro.

5. Meat Rich Stew

Prep: 15min/**Cook:** 30min/**Total:** 45min
Servings: 10/**Calories:** 207/**Fat:** 7.3g
Protein: 27.8g/**Carbs:** 6.5g

Ingredients:

- 3 ½ lbs. Chuck Roast, chopped into small cubes
- 1 sliced Onion
- 4 tbsp. of Garlic, minced
- 2 tsp. of Cumin
- 2 ½ tsp. of Oregano, dried
- 2 tsp. of Salt
- 2 tsp. of Paprika
- 1 tsp. of Smoked Paprika
- 1/8 tsp. of Cloves, grounded
- ½ tsp. of Black pepper
- 14 oz. of Tomatoes, diced
- 2-3 Bay leafs
- Green olives for garnish
- 3 mixed and sliced Bell peppers

Directions:

1. Add the ingredients in the pot except for the leafs and bell peppers.
2. Close the lid and let it cook for 25 minutes on high pressure.
3. Let the pressure release naturally.
4. Press sauté and add the mixed bell peppers. Cook for 5 minutes.
5. Add the leafs and stir.
6. Serve and enjoy!

6. Tender Juicy Meatballs

Prep: 15min/**Cook:** 20min/**Total:** 35min
Servings:5/**Calories:** 455/**Fat:** 33g
Protein: 34g/**Carbs:** 5g

Ingredients:
- 1 ½ lb. of ground Beef
- 2 tbsp. of Parsley, chopped
- ½ cup of Almond Flour
- ¾ cup of Parmesan, grated
- 2 eggs
- ¼ tsp. of Black pepper
- 1 tsp. of Salt
- 1 tsp. of Onion flakes, dried
- ¼ tsp. of Garlic powder
- ¼ tsp. of Oregano, dried
- 1/3 cup of Water, warm

For cooking:
- 3 cups of Marinara sauce (keto friendly)

- 1 tsp. of Olive oil

Directions:
1. In a bowl, combine the ingredients for the meatballs. Mix well by hand.
2. Now form meatballs. About 15.
3. Coat the instant pot with oil and brown them in batches until well browned on all sides.
4. Layer the meatballs in the pot; just leave about ½ inch space between each of them. Do not press them down.
5. Pour the sauce over them.
6. Close the pot and cook for 10 minutes on low pressure.
7. Let the pressure release naturally.
8. Serve these juicy meatballs with spaghetti squash or noodles and enjoy!

7. Cabbage and Beef

Prep: 5min/**Cook**: 30min/**Total:** 35min
Servings: 5/**Calories:** 295/**Fat:** 17g
Protein: 19g/**Carbs:** 4g

Ingredients:
- 2 ½ lb. of Corned beef cut into 3 pieces
- 1 Cabbage head
- 4 carrots, cleaned and cut into pieces
- 1 cup of Vegetable broth, low sodium
- 1 cup of Water
- 1 tbsp. of Garlic powder
- 1 tbsp. of Onion powder
- 1 tbsp. of Pepper flakes
- 1 tsp. of Dry mustard
- ½ tbsp. of Black pepper
- 1 tbsp. of Salt

Directions:
1. Place the beef pieces in the pot. Add water and add the seasonings.
2. Add the cabbage and the carrots.
3. Close the lid and cook for 30 minutes at high pressure.

4. Let the pressure release naturally.
5. Serve and enjoy!

8. Steak Bites

Prep: 5min/**Cook:** 14min/**Total:** 19min
Servings: 4/**Calories:** 430/**Fat:** 21.6g
Protein: 51.5g/**Carbs:** 4g

Ingredients:
- 2 lbs. of Beef Stew Meat
- ¼ tsp. of Salt
- 2 tsp. of Avocado oil
- 4 tbsp. of Steak seasoning
- 2 tbsp. of Ghee
- 1 Garlic clove, minced
- 1 tbsp. of Onion Flakes, dried
- 4 oz. of Mushrooms, sliced
- ½ cup of Bone Broth

Directions:
1. Turn on Sauté mode.

2. Add the oil, meat, mushrooms, and garlic. Cook for about 5 minutes. Make sure to stir frequently to avoid burning the garlic.

3. Add the remaining ingredients and stir.

4. Close the pot and cook for 9 minutes at high pressure.
5. Quick release the pressure.
6. Serve and enjoy!

Chapter 2 – Breakfast Recipes

1. Pepper Broccoli & Ham Frittata

Prep: 10 min/**Cook:** 30 min /**Total:** 40 min
Servings: 4**Calories:** 422/**Fat:** 30g
Protein: 28g/**Carbs:** 7g

Ingredients:

- 4 Eggs
- 2 cups of Broccoli, frozen
- 1 cup of sliced Sweet Peppers
- 8 oz. of Ham, cubed
- 1 cup of Heavy cream
- 1 tsp. of Salt
- 1 cup of Cheddar cheese, shredded
- 2 tsp. of Black pepper

Directions:

1. Grease a pan (6x3) very well.

2. Place the sweet pepper on the bottom.

3. Place the ham over the peppers.

4. Cover the sweet peppers and ham with broccoli.

5. In a bowl, beat the eggs and whisk in heavy cream, black pepper, and salt. Add the cheese and stir.

6. Pour the mixture on the ham and veggies. Cover with silicone lid or foil.

7. Pour 2 cups of water in the instant pot and place the steamer rack.

8. Position the pan over the rack and close the lid.

9. Cook for 20 minutes at high pressure. Release the pressure naturally for 10 minutes. Quickly release the remaining pressure.

10. Let it rest for 5-7 minutes outside the Instant Pot. Flip the pan on a plate and slice the frittata into serving sizes.

11. Serve and enjoy!

2. Egg Bake with Cheese

Prep: 6 min /**Cook:** 20 min/**Total:** 26 min
Servings: 4/**Calories:** 380/**Fat: 20g**
Protein: 33g/**Carbs**: 2.7g

Ingredients:
- 6 Bacon slices, chopped
- 6 eggs
- ¼ cup of cream
- 1 tsp. of Salt
- ½ cup of Cheddar cheese, shredded
- ½ tsp. of Pepper
- Optional: green onions, mushrooms, spinach, red pepper, and onion

Directions:
1. Cook the bacon in the instant pot until crispy.
2. Add optional veggies and sauté, until they become tender.
3. Oil a container that is heatproof, and that you can place inside the Instant Pot.
4. In a bowl, combine cream, eggs, black pepper, salt, and cheese. Whisk well and then add the veggies and bacon. Stir again.
5. Pour the mixture in the container.

6. Add 1 ½ cups of water into the instant pot and place a trivet inside. Place the container with the mixture.

7. Close the lid and cook for 20 min. at high pressure. Quick release the pressure.

8. Loosen the edges and flip the container onto a plate.

9. Serve with shredded cheese and green onions and enjoy!

3. Frittata with cheese

Prep: 10min/**Cook:** 20min/**Total:** 30min
Servings: 4/**Calories:** 257g/**Fat:** 19g
Protein: 14g/**Carbs:** 6g

Ingredients:
- 4 Eggs
- 10 oz. of Green Chiles, diced
- 1 cup of Heavy Cream
- ½ Tsp. of Cumin, ground
- ½ – 1 Tsp. of Salt
- ¼ cup of shredded cheese, Mexican Blend
- ¼ cup of Cilantro, chopped

Directions:

1. In a mixing bowl, beat the eggs and then add the ½ cup of the cheese blend, cumin, salt, green chilis, and heavy cream.

2. Pour the mixture in a greased silicon or metal pan (6 inches) and cover using a foil (Using glass means it will cook longer). Also, make sure to brush the pan with oil generously because eggs tend to stick a lot.

3. Pour 2 cups water in the Instant Pot and then place the trivet.

4. Place the pan.

5. Cook for 20 minutes under high pressure. Let the pressure release naturally for 10 minutes and then you can quick release the remaining pressure.

6. Now, scatter the remaining ½ cup of cheese blend on top and broil got 5 minutes.

7. Serve and enjoy!

4. Crustless Meat Quiche

Prep: 10min   /**Cook:** 30min/**Total:** 40min
Servings: 4/**Calories:** 323/**Fat:** 22g
Protein: 17g/**Carbs:** 9g

Ingredients:
- 6 eggs, beaten
- Black pepper and salt to taste
- ½ cup of cream
- 4 bacon slices, cooked and then crumbled
- 1 cup of Ground sausage, cooked
- 1 cup of Diced ham

- 1 cup of cheese, shredded
- 2 chopped green onion

Directions:

1. Take one cup of water and pour it into the instant pot and place a trivet on the bottom.

2. Now, in a bowl, combine the cream, eggs, black pepper and salt. Add the sausage, bacon, ham, cheese and green onions in a soufflé dish (1 quart). Pour the egg mixture in the dish, and stir.

3. Cover the dish loosely with foil, and make a foil slink to help you place the soufflé dish inside the pot.

4. Close the lid and let it cook for 30 minutes at high pressure. Let the pressure release naturally for 10 minutes and then quick release the rest of the pressure.

5. Open the lid, take the dish out and discard the foil.

6. Sprinkle with cheese and then broil until lightly browned and melted.

5. Egg Muffins

Prep: 10min/**Cook:** 8min/**Total:** 18 min
Servings: 4/**Calories:** 380/**Fat:** 37g
Protein: 26g/**Carbs:** 2g

Ingredients:
- 4 Eggs
- 4 tbsp. of Jack or cheddar cheese, shredded
- 1 -2 green onions, diced
- 4 bacon slices, crumbled, precooked

Directions:

1. Put a steamer basket inside the instant pot and then pour 1 ½ cups of water.

2. In a measuring bowl, break the eggs and add the lemon pepper. Beat well.

3. Divide the green onion, bacon, and cheese into muffin cups (silicone). Pour the eggs in each cup and then stir to combine.

4. Place the cups on the basket, cover and cook for 8 minutes at high pressure. Once done quick release the pressure (let it sit first for 2 minutes).

5. Open and lift the basket. Remove the cups.

6. Serve right away

6. Simple Casserole

Prep: 5/**Cook:** 20/**Total:** 25
Servings: 5-6/**Calories:** 289/**Fat:** 20g
Protein: 27g/**Carbs:** 5g

Ingredients:

- 32 oz. of frozen peas
- 1-2 cups of Crumbled, Sausage (turkey)
- 1 Onion, large, diced
- 2 cups of Cheddar cheese, shredded
- 1 cup of cream
- 12 Eggs, Large

- 1 tsp. of black pepper
- 1 tsp. of Salt

Directions:

1. Spray your instant pot with a cooking spray, and add the peas.

2. Top with 1/3 Sausage, 1/3 onion, and 1/3 cheese. Repeat this 2 times.

3. In a bowl, combine the cream, eggs, black pepper, and salt. Whisk until blended.

4. Pour over the ingredients already in the instant pot.

5. Close the lid and cook for 20 minutes at high pressure.

6. Quick release the pressure.

7. Scoop onto plates and serve with desired toppings.

7. Asparagus Frittata

Prep: 10 min/**Cook:** 20 min/**Total:** 35 min
Servings: 4/**Calories:** 238/**Fat:** 19g
Protein: 14g/**Carbs:** 5g

Ingredients:
- 6 Eggs
- 1 tbsp. of Butter
- ½ cup of chopped Green Onions
- ½ lb. of Asparagus, trimmed, cut into smaller 2-3 pieces
- ½ cup of Swiss Cheese
- ¼ cup of Heavy Cream
- Black pepper and salt to taste

Directions:

1. First, steam the asparagus in a bowl with 2 tbsp. of Water and covered. Place in the microwave for 2 minutes.

2. In a bowl, beat the eggs and add the heavy cream, cheese, black pepper, and salt.

3. Now melt the butter in a skillet over medium heat.

4. Add the green onions and cook 1 minute. Add the asparagus, black pepper and salt to taste.

5. Add the green onions and asparagus into the egg mixture. Pour into a baking tray that can fit inside the instant pot.

6. Add 1 ½ cup of water in the instant pot and place a trivet. Position the tray on the trivet. Close the instant pot and cook at high pressure for 20 minutes.

7. Once done quick release the pressure.

8. Serve and enjoy!

8. Egg Cups

Prep: 5min/**Cook:** 10min/**Total:** 15min
Servings: 4/**Calories:** 115/**Fat:** 9g
Protein: 9g/**Carbs:** 2g

Ingredients:
- 4 Eggs
- ½ cup of Cheddar Cheese, shredded
- 1 cup of Veggies, diced (like tomatoes, mushrooms, bell peppers, and onions)
- ¼ cup of Heavy Cream
- 2 tbsp. of Cilantro, chopped
- ½ cup of Cheese, shredded (for the finish)
- Black pepper and salt to taste

Directions:
1. In a bowl, combine the cilantro, black pepper, salt, heavy cream, cheese, veggies, and eggs. Whisk well and then divide the mixture into 4 jars, wide mouth (1/2 pint), or containers of your choice. Close them, but not very tightly in order to keep the water away from the eggs.

2. Pour 2 cups of water inside the Instant Pot and position the trivet.

3. Place the jars.

4. Cook at high pressure for 5 minutes. Release the pressure quickly.

5. Top the egg cups with ½ cup of cheese. Now place them in an air fryer for 2-3 minutes, or broil them.

6. Serve and enjoy!

9. Breakfast Sandwich

Prep: 10min/**Cook:** 20min/**Total**: 30min
Servings: 1/**Calories:** 760/**Fat:** 52.5 g
Protein: 52.3g/**Carbs:** 2.5g

Ingredients:

- 6 oz. of 1 skinless, boneless Chicken breast
- 1/8 tsp. of Black pepper
- ¼ tsp. of Salt
- 2 tbsp. of Coconut oil
- ¼ tsp. of Garlic powder
- 1 cup of water
- 1 Egg
- 2 tbsp. of Mayonnaise

- – ¼ Avocado
- ¼ cup of white Cheddar, Shredded

Directions:

1. Cut the breast lengthwise into half. Pound the chicken until thin. Season with garlic powder, pepper, and salt. Set aside.

2. Add coconut oil (1 tbsp.) into the pot and press sauté. Set "less" for temperature. Once hot, cook the egg. Set aside.

3. Now, press cancel and press sauté again. Adjust temperature to Normal. Add the remaining coconut oil and cook the chicken for 4 minutes on both sites.

4. Now close the lid, and cook for 7-8 minutes at high pressure.

5. In the meantime, mash the avocado and stir in the mayo.

6. Once the chicken is cooked, release the pressure quickly. Transfer the chicken into a plate, and then use a paper towel to pat dry it.

7. Use the chicken breasts as buns, and assemble a sandwich: place one piece on a plate, place the avocado mayo, cheese and egg. Season lightly with black pepper and salt. Serve and enjoy!

10. Blueberry Muffins

Prep: 5/**Cook:** 30/**Total:** 35
Servings: 6/**Calories:** 89/**Fat:** 3g
Protein: 3g/**Carbs:** 2g

Ingredients:
- 1/3 cup of Coconut Flour
- 4 ½ tsp. of Erythritol Sweetener
- 1 ½ tbsp. of Flaxseed meal, golden
- 1/8 tsp. of Sea salt
- ¼ tsp. of Baking Soda
- 1 tsp. of Baking powder
- 2 Eggs, beaten (large)
- 1/3 cup of Almond Milk, unsweetened
- 1 tsp. of Vanilla extract
- 1 ½ tbsp. of melted Butter
- 1/3 cup of Blueberries, fresh

Directions:

1. In a bowl, combine the flaxseed meal, coconut flour, baking soda, baking powder, sweetener, and salt. Mix well to break clumps. Set aside.

2. Separately, mix eggs, almond milk, vanilla extract, and melted butter. Mix well.

3. Add wet mixture into the dry pot. Mix until there are no clumps. Add the blueberries and fold gently. Set aside.

4. Add 1 cup water into the Instant Pot.

5. Fill silicone cupcake liners (fill ¾). Because the butter is pretty thick, you should press the butter down with the fingers.

6. Place a foil on the steamer and then place the cups. Fold the excess foil over the cups. Lower the steamer rack in the pot.

7. Cover the muffins with a second foil.

8. Close the lid and let it cook for 20 minutes at High pressure.

9. Release the pressure naturally for 10 minutes. Then, quick release the pressure.

10. Open and remove the foil. Lift the rack and transfer the cups onto serving plates.

11. Serve and enjoy!

Chapter 3 – Fish and Sea Food

1. Tomato Sauce Scallops

Prep: 10min/**Cook:** 13min/**Total:** 23min
Servings: 4/**Calories:** 74/**Fat:** 3g
Protein: 2g/**Carbs:** 7g

Ingredients:
- 1 ½ lb. of Scallops, fresh, cleaned
- 2 tbsp. of Olive oil
- 1 Onion, diced
- 1 Garlic clove, minced
- 3 ½ cups of Tomatoes, fresh, peeled
- 6 oz. of Tomato paste
- 2 tbsp. of Italian parsley, chopped
- ¼ cup of red wine
- 1 tbsp. of fresh oregano, chopped
- Black pepper and salt to taste

Directions:

1. Turn on sauté and add the oil.

2. Once heated, add the garlic and onion. Cook for 3 minutes. Add the parsley, wine, oregano, tomato paste, and tomatoes. Season with black pepper and salt. Mix well.

3. Close the lid and cook for 8 minutes, at high pressure.

4. Once done quick release the pressure. Taste the sauce and adjust seasoning if needed.

5. Turn on sauté again, and add the scallop. Cook for 1 minute. Once it starts to simmer, cancel the function.

6. Now close the lid and let it rest for 8 minutes so that the scallops can be perfectly cooked.

7. Serve and enjoy!

2. Simple and tasty Clams

Prep: 5min/**Cook:** 4min/**Total:** 9min
Servings: 4/**Calories:** 138/**Fat:** 2g
Protein: 23g/**Carbs:** 4g

Ingredients:

- 4 lbs. of Clams
- 1 cup of White wine
- 1 tsp. of minced Garlic
- ½ cup of chopped Parsley
- 1 cup of water

Directions:
1. Add parsley, garlic, and wine in the instant pot.
2. Add water and place steam basked. Add the clams.
3. Close the lid and cook at high pressure for 4 minutes.
4. Serve with the juice from the pot and enjoy!

3. Teriyaki Salmon

Prep: 10min/**Cook**: 3min/**Total:** 13min
Servings: 4/**Calories**: 315/**Fat:** 35g
Protein: 37g/**Carbs:** 5g

Ingredients:
- 1 cup of peas, frozen
- 4 salmon fillets, small
- 2 ginger slices, diced
- 2 garlic cloves, sliced
- ½ red chili, long, sliced
- Seas salt, a pinch
- ¼ cup of Teriyaki sauce

Directions:

1. Add water (1 cup) in the pot, and place the trivet. Add the frozen peas in a round tin that can fit in the pot. Place the fish and sprinkle with chili, garlic, ginger, and salt. Drizzle with teriyaki.

2. Close the lid and choose "steam," and adjust to 3 min. Once done quick release the pressure.

3. Open the lid and take the tin out.

4. Serve the salmon filets as they are with peas, or you can also add zucchini noodles or cauliflower rice.

5. Enjoy!

4. Fish Curry

Prep: 5min/**Cook:** 10min/**Total**: 15min
Servings: 4/**Calories**: 190/**Fat:** 11g
Protein: 16g/**Carbs:** 4g

Ingredients:
- 1 ½ lb. of Cod, cut into pieces
- 1 tsp. of fresh lime juice
- 1 cup of coconut milk
- 2 tbsp. of Water
- Black pepper and salt to taste
- ½ tsp. of Turmeric
- ¼ tsp. of Cumin, grounded
- 1 tsp. of Coriander, grounded
- 1 cup of chopped Tomato
- ½ chili pepper, slit
- 1 tbsp. of minced Ginger
- 1 tbsp. of minced Garlic
- 1 cup of chopped onion
- Optional: 7 curry leaves

- 2 tbsp. of coconut oil
- For garnish: Cilantro (optional)
- For garnish: Tomato slices (optional)

Directions:

1. Turn on sauté mode. Add oil and add the curry leaves. Cook for 20 seconds.
2. Add chilies, ginger, garlic, and onions. Cook for 3-4 minutes.
3. Add the tomatoes and cook for 5 more minutes.
4. Add salt, black pepper, turmeric, cumin, and coriander.
5. Sauté for 30 seconds.
6. Deglaze with 2 tbsp. of Water and add the coconut milk. Add the fish and make sure that the milk is under and over the fish.
7. Close the pot and cook at high pressure for 20 minutes.
8. Quick release the pressure, and add the lime juice.
9. Stir carefully. Again, gently remove the gravy and fish, and serve in bowls.
10. Garnish with tomato slices and cilantro over cauliflower rice. Enjoy!

5. Lemon Salmon

Prep: 3min/**Cook:** 17min/**Total:** 20min
Servings: 3-4/**Calories:** 280/**Fat:** 20g
Protein: 20g/**Carbs:** 7g

Ingredients:
- 1 ½ lb. of Salmon filets, frozen
- ¾ cup of Water
- ¼ cup of Lemon juice
- A mix of fresh parsley, basil, and dill (few sprigs)
- ¼ tsp. of Garlic powder
- ¼ tsp. of Salt
- Black pepper to taste
- 1 tbsp. of Coconut oil or avocado oil
- 1 lemon, thinly sliced.

Directions:
1. Pour the lemon juice and water into the pot. Add the fresh herbs. Place a steamer rack.
2. Season the salmon with black pepper and salt and drizzle oil.
3. Sprinkle with garlic powder and place the salmon on the rack in one layer.

4. Place the lemon slices.
5. Close the lid.
6. Cook for 7 minutes at high pressure.
7. Once done, quick release the pressure.
8. Enjoy this lemon salmon with veggies.

6. Coconut Shrimp

Prep: 10min/**Cook:** 10min/**Total:** 20min
Servings: 4/**Calories:** 190/**Fat:** 12g
Protein: 16g/**Carbs:** 3g

Ingredients:
- 1 lb. of Shrimps, divined
- 1 tbsp. of Garlic, minced
- 1 tbsp. of Ginger, minced
- ½ tsp. of Turmeric
- 1 tsp. of Salt
- 1 tsp. of Garam Masala
- ½ Tsp. of Cayenne pepper
- 1 cup of Coconut milk

Directions:
1. In a bowl, combine all ingredients. Mix well.
2. In the pot, add water (2 cups), and then place the trivet.
3. In a pot that can fit inside the pot, add the mixture and clover using a foil.
4. Place the pot inside the instant pot and the cook at low pressure for 4 minutes. Quick release the pressure.
5. Serve as it is, or with cauliflower rice.

7. Creamy Shrimp

Prep: 5min/**Cook**: 10min/**Total:** 15min
Servings: 6/**Calories:** 315/**Fat:** 9g
Protein: 24g/**Carbs:** 2g

Ingredients:

- 1 lb. of Shrimp, frozen
- 2 tbsp. of Butter
- 4 Garlic cloves, minced
- ½ tsp. of Paprika
- ½ tsp. of Pepper flakes
- 2 Zucchini, cut into noodles
- 1 cup of Chicken broth
- ½ cup of parmesan cheese
- ½ cup of Heavy cream
- Black pepper and salt to taste

Directions:

1. Turn on sauté and add the butter.
2. Add pepper flakes and garlic. Cook for 1 minute.

3. Add the shrimp, paprika, black pepper, and salt.
4. Pour the broth.
5. Cook at high pressure for 2 minutes.
6. Quick release the pressure and open the pot.
7. Add the cheese and heavy cream. Stir to melt. Add the zucchini noodles.
8. Serve and enjoy!

Chapter 4 – Vegetable and Bean Dishes

1. Zucchini Noodles

Prep: 5min/**Cook:** 2min/**Total:** 7min
Servings: 2/**Calories:** 20/**Fat:** 0.3g
Protein: 1.2g/**Carbs:** 2g
Ingredients:

- 2 Zucchinis, large, spiralized
- 2 Garlic Cloves
- ½ lemon, the juice
- 2 tbsp. of Parmesan, grated
- 2 tbsp. of Olive oil
- Black pepper and salt to taste

Directions:
1. Add oil into the pot and turn on sauté.
2. Add the garlic and cook for 1 minute.
3. Add the lemon juice, zucchinis and season with black pepper and salt.
4. Cook for 30 seconds, until firm and crispy.
5. Mix well. Serve with Parmesan cheese and enjoy!

2. Spaghetti Squash

Prep: 5min/**Cook**: 5min/**Total:** 10min
Servings: 6/**Calories:** 20/**Fat:** 0
Protein: 1g/**Carbs:** 4g

Ingredients:

- 1 Squash, spaghetti
- 1 cup of Water
- Black pepper and salt

Directions:

1. Cut the squash lengthwise. Discard the seeds.
2. Place the 2 pieces in the pot and pour water.
3. Close the lid and cook for 5 minutes at high pressure.
4. Quick release the pressure.
5. Transfer the squash pieces on a plate and use a fork to make "spaghetti".
6. Season with black pepper and salt.

3. Creamed Spinach

Prep: 3min/**Cook:** 10min/**Total:** 13min
Servings: 4/**Calories:** 165/**Fat:** 15g
Protein: 3g/**Carbs:** 4g

Ingredients:
- 1 lb. of Baby spinach, raw
- 4 Garlic cloves, sliced
- 2 tbsp. of Ghee
- ½ Tsp. of Himalayan salt
- ½ tsp. of Black pepper
- 1/8 tsp. of Nutmeg
- 8 oz. of Cream cheese

Directions:

1. Turn on sauté mode. Once heated add the ghee.

2. Add garlic and add the spinach. Cover the instant pot (don't close it, no pressure) and let it cook for 3 minutes.

3. Open and stir. Season with black pepper, nutmeg, and salt.

4. Once wilted, stir more until the leaves become dark green.

5. Once the liquid evaporates add the cream cheese. Cook until creamy.

6. Serve and enjoy!

4. Cabbage Rice

Prep: 10min/**Cook:** 5min/**Total:** 15min
Servings: 6/**Calories:** 47/**Fat:** 0
Protein: 2g/**Carbs:** 6g

Ingredients:
- 1 Cabbage head, shredded (riced)
- 1 tbsp. of Turmeric
- 2 tbsp. of Ghee
- ½ Tsp. of Curry powder

- Black pepper and salt to taste
- 3 Garlic cloves, minced

Directions:

1. Turn on sauté and melt the ghee. Add black pepper, salt, garlic, curry, and turmeric.

2. Add the cabbage. Stir until coated.

3. Close the lid and cook for 5 minutes at high pressure.

4. Quick release the pressure.

5. Serve and enjoy!

5. Mashed Cauliflower

Prep: 5min/**Cook:** 8min/**Total:** 15min
Servings: 4/**Calories:** 235/**Fat:** 19g
Protein: 12g/**Carbs:** 1g

Ingredients:

- 1 Cauliflower head (large), broken into florets and cored
- 1 ½ cups of water
- 1 Garlic clove
- ½ tsp. of Butter
- 1 tbsp. of Sour cream
- ¼ tsp. of Mustard powder, dry (optional
- Black pepper and salt to taste
- ¼ cup of Parmesan cheese, grated
- ¾ cup of Cheddar cheese, fat-free
- 4 bacon sliced, cooked until crisp and then diced
- 2 sliced green onion for garnish

Directions:

1. Preheat the oven, 375°F.

2. Place a steamer basket in the pot.

3. Place the cauliflower florets in the basket.

4. Close and cook for 3 minutes at high pressure.

5. Quick release the pressure.

6. Blend the cauliflower in a blender or food processor until smooth.

7. Add black pepper, salt, mustard, sour cream butter, and garlic. Process again.

8. Transfer the mashed cauliflower in a baking pan.

9. Top with bacon and cheeses.

10. Bake for 5 minutes.

11. Sprinkle with sliced green onions and serve.

6. Brussels Sprouts

Prep: 3min/**Cook:** 3min/**Total:** 6min
Servings: 4/**Calories:** 150/**Fat:** 20g
Protein: 7g/**Carbs:** 5g

Ingredients:

- 1 lb. of Brussels Sprouts
- ¼ cup of Pine Nuts
- Black pepper and salt to taste
- Olive oil

Directions:

1. In the pot, place a trivet and place a steamer basket.

2. Pour 1 cup of water.

3. Add Brussels sprouts in the basket.

4. Close the lid and cook for 3 minutes at high pressure.

5. Quick release the pressure.

6. Season with black pepper and salt; drizzle with olive oil and sprinkle Pine Nuts. Serve and enjoy!

7. Green Beans

Prep: 5min/**Cook:** 3min/**Total:** 8min
Servings: 4/**Calories:** 95/**Fat:** 4.5g
Protein: 6g/**Carbs:** 5g

Ingredients:

- 1lb. of Green Beans
- 1 tbsp. of Butter
- ¼ cup of Bacon, cooked and chopped
- Black pepper and salt to taste

Directions:

1. Trim the ends of the beans and wash them.

2. Now, add 1-cup of water into the pot and place a steamer.

3. Add the bacon pieces and green beans into the steamer and close the lid of your Instant Pot.

4. Turn on high-pressure and let it cook for 3 minutes.

5. Quick release the pressure and open the pot. Add the butter and stir. It will melt easily.

6. Serve!

Chapter 5 – Soups & Stews

1. Spinach Pork Stew

Prep: 10min/**Cook:** 30min/**Total:** 40min
Servings: 4/**Calories:** 290/**Fat:** 17g
Protein: 23g/**Carbs:** 9g

Ingredients:
- 1lb. of Pork butt, cut into small chunks (2 inches)
- 4 Garlic Cloves
- 10 oz. of chopped tomatoes
- 1 tsp. of dried Thyme
- 2 tsp. of Cajun blend seasoning
- 1 Onion
- 4-6 cups of Baby Spinach, chopped
- ½ cup of Heavy Cream

Directions:

1. In a blender, blend the tomatoes, garlic, and onion.

2. Pour the mixture into the pot and add the Cajun seasoning.

3. Add the pork and stir.

4. Close, turn on MEAT setting, and cook for 20 minutes. Let the pressure release naturally, 10 minutes. Quickly release the remaining pressure.

5. Turn on sauté. Once it starts to boil, add the cream and spinach. Stir and turn off sautéing. Let it rest for a few minutes.

6. Serve and enjoy!

2. Pork Stew

Prep: 15min/**Cook:** 30min/**Total:** 45min
Servings: 12/**Calories:** 290/**Fat:** 25g
Protein: 10g/**Carbs:** 2g

Ingredients:

- 4 lbs. of Country-style ribs, boneless; cut into small cubes
- 2 of tbsp. Butter
- 2 tbsp. of Oil
- Black pepper and salt to taste
- Garlic powder to taste
- ¾ cup of Apple Cider vinegar
- ¾ cup of Beef broth
- 1 medium Cabbage, julienned
- ½ cup of Green onion
- 3 shredded Carrots
- 1 cup of Whipping cream

Directions:

1. Turn on sauté and add the butter. Once heated, add the pork and brown it. Set aside.

2. Deglaze the bottom with broth and vinegar. Once it starts to simmer add the meat and add the remaining ingredients and seasoning (except cream).

3. Close the lid and cook for 30 minutes at high pressure.

4. Let the pressure release naturally.

5. Stir in the cream and turn on sauté just to heat it.

6. Serve and enjoy!

3. Beef Veggie Soup

Prep: 20min/**Cook:** 20min/**Total:** 40min
Servings: 8/**Calories:** 400/**Fat:** 23g
Protein: 28g/**Carbs:** 8g

Ingredients:
- 4 tbsp. of Ghee or avocado oil
- 1 Onion, diced
- 3 cups of diced Celeriac (peeled)
- 4 diced Carrots
- 4 Celery stalks, diced
- 15 oz. of diced tomatoes
- 2 lbs. of Ground beef
- 4 cups of beef/chicken broth
- 1 tsp. of White pepper
- 2 tsp. of Garlic powder
- 1 tsp. of Onion powder
- 2 tsp. of Herbs Provence
- 1 tbsp. of Salt

- ¾ cup of Green peas, frozen

Directions:

1. Turn on sauté and let the ghee melt.
2. Add celery, carrots celeriac root and onion. Sauté for 5-10 minutes, stirring frequently.
3. Add the ground beef and cook for 5 more minutes.
4. Close the pot and cook for 20 minutes at high pressure.
5. Release the pressure manually once finished cooking.
6. Stir in the peas and let it sit for 5 minutes before you serve into bowls.
7. Serve and enjoy!

4. Bacon Chicken Chowder

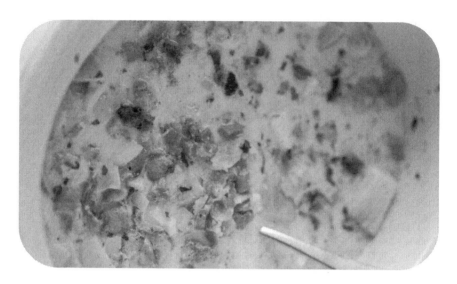

Prep: 10min/**Cook:** 30min /**Total:** 40min
Servings: 4-6/**Calories:** 260/**Fat:** 34g
Protein: 28g/**Carbs:** 5g

Ingredients:
- 6 Chicken thighs, boneless
- 8 oz. of full fat Cream Cheese
- 4 tsp. of Garlic, minced
- 1 cup of Celery and onion mix, chopped (frozen)
- 6 oz. of Mushrooms, sized
- 4 tbsp. of Butter
- 1 tsp. of thyme
- Black pepper and salt to taste
- 3 cups of Chicken broth
- 1 lb. of Bacon, cooked, chopped
- 1 cup of Heavy Cream
- 2 cups of Spinach, fresh

Directions:
1. In the instant pot, add all ingredients except the bacon, cream, and the spinach.

2. Close the lid and set at soup mode.
3. Once done, quick release pressure.
4. Stir in the cream and spinach.
5. Ladle into bowls and top with bacon, enjoy!

5. Chicken Soup

Prep: 10min/**Cook:** 20min/**Total:** 30min
Servings: 8/**Calories:** 190/**Fat:** 10g
Protein: 26g /**Carbs**: 5g

Ingredients:
- 10 cups of Chicken stock or Bone Broth
- ½ tsp. of Oregano, dried
- ½ tsp. of Garlic powder
- 1 cup Celery, thinly sliced
- 1 ½ cups of Butternut squash, diced
- 2 Chicken breasts
- 2 cups of Jicama, chopped into thinly pieces like "rice" (peeled)
- 1 tbsp. of Cider vinegar apple
- Black pepper and salt to taste

Directions:
1. In the instant pot combine all ingredients.
2. Close the lid and set to high pressure for 20 minutes.
3. Once done, naturally release the pressure for about 10 minutes and then quick release.

4. Open the lid and transfer the chicken breasts on to a cutting board. Cube or shred the chicken and return to the pot. Stir well.

5. Add cider vinegar and parsley; season with black pepper and salt to taste.

6. Serve and enjoy!

6. Cheeseburger Soup

Prep: 15min/**Cook:** 15min/**Total:** 30min
Servings: 6/**Calories:** 607/Fat: 47g
Protein: 33g/**Carbs:** 8g

Ingredients:
- 1 ½ lb. of Hamburger
- 6 oz. of chopped Bacon
- 1 Onion, diced
- 4 cups of chopped Cauliflower
- 2 Celery stalks, diced
- 2 Carrots, diced
- 4 cups of Chicken or Beef broth
- 4 oz. of Cream Cheese
- Sea salt to taste
- 1 cup of Cheddar cheese, sharp (or to taste)

Directions:
1. Turn on sauté and brown the bacon. Set aside.
2. Add the beef and brown until cooked. Set aside.

3. Add the veggies, sauté for few minutes and add the broth.

4. Close the lid and cook for 7 minutes at high pressure.

5. Quick release the pressure.

6. Cook Puree the soup with an immersion blender directly in the instant pot.

7. Add the cheese and blend again.

8. Add the hamburger and bacon, stir. Let it rest for 5-10 minutes.

9. Serve and enjoy!

7. Noodle Soup

Prep: 10min/**Cook:** 25min/**Total:** 35min
Servings: 6/**Calories:** 164/**Fat:** 5g
Protein: 19g/**Carbs:** 8g

Ingredients:

- 1 skinless, boneless Chicken breasts, seasoned with black pepper and salt or seasoning of your choice
- 1 tbsp. of Olive oil + Rosemary
- 1 diced Red Onion
- 3 sliced, Carrots
- 3 diced, Celery ribs
- 1 diced, Banana pepper
- 1 diced, Jalapeno, pepper (optional)
- 2 cloves of garlic, minced
- Black pepper and salt to taste
- 1-2 bay leaves
- 6 cups of Chicken broth, fat-free, low sodium
- 2 tbsp. of cider vinegar, apple
- 4 Zucchini, spiralized

Directions:

1. In the instant pot, drizzle 1 tbsp. of Olive oil and turn on sauté.

2. Once heated, add garlic, peppers, celery, carrots, and onions; season with black pepper and salt. Cook for 4 minutes until tender.

3. Add the cider vinegar and chicken broth.

4. Close the instant pot.

5. Cook at high pressure for 15 minutes. Once done, let the pressure release naturally for 10 minutes, and then quick release the remaining pressure.

6. Remove the chicken on a board and shred it. Transfer back into the pot and add the spiralized zucchini.

7. Press sauté and cook for 5 minutes.

8. Serve into bowls, drizzled with olive oil with rosemary.

8. Chicken Buffalo Simple Soup

Prep: 10min /**Cook:** 20min/**Total:** 30min
Servings: 6/**Calories:** 270/**Fat:** 23g
Protein: 55g/**Carbs:** 6g

Ingredients:
- 1 lb. of cooked Chicken, shredded
- 1 tbsp. of Olive oil
- 4 Garlic cloves, minced
- ½ cup of Celery, diced
- ½ Onion, diced
- 4 cups of Chicken broth
- 2-3 tbsp. of Buffalo Sauce
- ½ cup of Heavy Cream
- 6 oz. of Cream Cheese (room temperature)

Directions:
1. Turn on sauté. Add the onion, celery, and oil. Cook for 5 minutes.
2. Now, add the garlic and cook for 1 minute. Turn off sauté.

3. Add buffalo sauce, broth, and chicken. Cover the pot and turn on soup mode for 5 minutes.

5. After it is done cooking, let the pressure release naturally for 5 minutes and then quick release it.

6. Ladle 1 cup of the soup liquid and pour it into a blender. Add cream cheese and puree until it becomes smooth.

7. About the cream cheese mixture in the pot and add the heavy cream. Stir.

8. Serve and enjoy!

9. Chicken Enchilada Simple Soup

Prep: 5min /**Cook:** 25min /**Total:** 30min
Servings: 4/**Calories:** 268/**Fat:** 11g
Protein: 30g/**Carbs:** 8.5g

Ingredients:
- 1 lb. of boneless, skinless Chicken breasts
- 1 tbsp. of Olive oil
- 1 diced yellow Onion
- 3 Garlic cloves, minced
- 1 diced Bell pepper
- 1 jalapeno, minced
- 8 fl. oz. of Tomato sauce, sugar-free
- 1 tbsp. of Chili powder
- 3 cups of Chicken broth
- 1 tsp. of Garlic powder
- 1 tbsp. of Chipotle pepper, adobo sauce
- 1 tsp. of Onion powder
- 1 tsp. of Wine vinegar, white
- ½ Tsp. of Oregano

- 1 tsp. of Sea salt

Optional Toppings:
- Cilantro, minced
- Sour Cream
- Jalapeno pepper, sliced
- Avocado, diced

Directions:
1. Add the oil into the pot and turn on Sauté. Add the bell pepper, garlic, jalapeno pepper, and onion. Cook for 4 minutes.

2. In a bowl, combine the spices, chipotle chili, vinegar, and tomato sauce. Pour in the instant pot.

3. Add the chicken and broth, stir. Close the lid. Cook 20 minutes at high pressure. Once done, quick release the pressure.

4. Take out the chicken, and shred. Transfer back into the pot.

5. Serve with toppings of your choice and enjoy!

10. Best and Simple Beef Stew

Prep: 15min /**Cook:** 30min/**Total:** 45min
Servings: 8/**Calories:** 514/**Fat:** 35g
Protein: 34g/**Carbs:** 8g

Ingredients:
- 2.6 lb. of Beef for stew or brisket
- 1 Onion, chopped
- 2 Garlic cloves, minced
- 1 Rutabaga, diced (peeled)
- 3 Turnips, kohlrabi, diced (peeled)
- 4 Stalks of Celery, chopped
- 2 tbsp. of duck fat or ghee
- Sea salt to taste
- 1 tbsp. of Paprika
- ½ tsp. of Black pepper
- ¼ tsp. of Allspice, grounded
- 14 oz. of fresh Tomatoes, chopped
- ½ cup of water
- 8 Egg yolks, large
- ¼ cup of Parsley, chopped

Directions:

1. Mince garlic and chop onion. Cut the beef into 1 ½ inch pieces. Set them aside.

2. Peel the kohlrabi and rutabaga cut them into small pieces and then chop the stalks of celery. Set aside.

3. Turn on sauté and add the ghee. Add the chopped onion. Cook for 3 minutes and then add garlic. Cook 30 seconds.

4. Add the meat. Season with black pepper and salt. Cook for 3 minutes.

5. Add celery, kohlrabi, chopped rutabaga, allspice, and paprika. Mix well and turn off sauté mode.

6. Close the pot and let it cook 30 minutes at high pressure. Thereafter, let the pressure release naturally for 15-20min and then quick release.

7. Make the cream sauce by whisking ½ cup water and yolks.

8. Strain the stew (red juices) into a saucepan. Simmer. Pour the simmering sauce in the yolk mixture while whisking constantly.

9. Once you pour half of the sauce, pour the red sauce and yolk mixture into the remaining simmering sauce. Cook for 5 minutes, stirring constantly.

10. Pour the sauce in the pot and stir.

11. Serve right away, topped with parsley.

Chapter 6 – Poultry Recipes

1. Chicken Meatballs

Prep: 10min/**Cook:** 20min/**Total:** 30min
Servings: 6/**Calories:** 357/**Fat:** 28g
Protein: 23g/**Carbs:** 2g

Ingredients:

- 1.5 lb. of Chicken, grounded
- 1 tsp. of Salt
- 3/4 cup of Almond meal
- 2 Cloves of garlic, minced
- 2 tbsp. of Ghee
- 2-3 green onions, sliced thinly
- 6 tbsp. of Hot sauce
- 4 tbsp. of butter or ghee
- For garnish: green onions, chopped

Directions:

1. In a bowl combine green onion, garlic, salt, almond meal, and chicken.

2. Mix everything well with your hands, but don't overwork the ground chicken.

3. Grease the hands with oil or ghee and shape balls, about 1 to 2 inches in size.

4. Turn on sauté mode and add ghee (2 tbsp.)

5. Brown the meatballs until the sides are browned. Work in batches.

6. In the meantime, combine 4 tbsp. of butter and hot sauce. Heat them on the stove or in the microwave until melted. Stir. This is the sauce.

7. Place the meatballs in the pot and pour the sauce.

8. Close the lid and turn on "poultry" mode.

9. Quick release the pressure if you are searching right away.

10. Serve with noodles or cauliflower rice and enjoy!

2. Juicy Simple Chicken Breasts

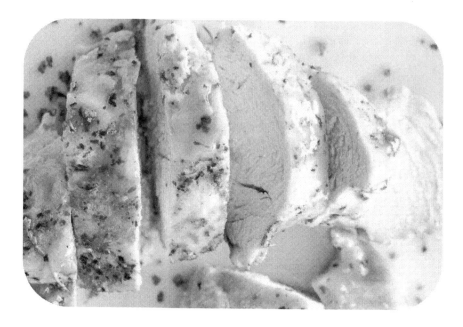

Prep: 2min/**Cook:** 20min /**Total:** 22min
Servings: 3/**Calories:** 170g/**Fat:** 7g
Protein: 24g/**Carbs:** 0

Ingredients:
- 1 tbsp. of Oil
- 3 skinless, boneless Chicken breasts
- ¼ Tsp. per breast Garlic salt
- Black pepper to taste
- 1/8 tsp. of Oregano, dried
- 1/8 tsp. of Basil, dried
- 1 cup of Water

Directions:
1. Turn on sauté and once heated, add the oil.
2. Season the breasts, just one side.
3. After the instant pot is hot, add the breasts with the seasoned side facing down.
4. Season the other side.
5. Cook for 4 minutes each side, and set aside.

6. Pour 1 cup of water in the pot and add the trivet.

7. Place the breasts.

8. Close the lid and cook for 5 minutes at high pressure.

9. Let the pressure release naturally for 5 minutes, and then you can quick release the remaining pressure.

10. Remove the breasts and wait for 5 minutes before you serve. This will provide maximum juiciness.

3. The Perfect Chicken Wings

Prep: 5min/**Cook:** 20 min/**Total:** 25min
Servings: 6/**Calories:** 430/**Fat:** 35g
Protein: 34g/**Carbs:** 1g

Ingredients:
- 5-6 lbs. of Chicken Wings
- 1 Cup of Hot sauce
- ¼ cup of Cider vinegar, apple
- 1 tsp. of Salt
- 1 tsp. of Black pepper
- 1 tbsp. of Ghee
- 1 tbsp. of Cayenne Pepper
  Extra Sauce Coating:
- 2 tbsp. of Ghee
- ½ cup of Hot Sauce

Directions:

1. Combine the first ingredients (not the wings) in a bowl and stir. Keep ¼ cup for coating and basting.

2. In the instant pot combine the sauce and chicken. Mix well.

3. Cook at high pressure for 10 minutes.

4. In the meantime, line a baking sheet with baking paper.

5. Once done, let the pressure release naturally.

6. Place the wings in one layer in the baking sheet, paste them with the reserved sauce and broil for 5 minutes. Turn them, and broil for 5 more minutes.

7. Make an extra sauce with the 2 ingredients.

8. Once the chicken is done serve the wings with the extra sauce. Serve with veggies of choice.

4. Crack Chicken

Prep: 5min/**Cook:** 20min/**Total:** 25min
Servings: 8/**Calories:** 443/**Fat:** 27.5g
Protein: 41.2g/**Carbs:** 4.3g

Ingredients:
- 2 lbs. of skinless, boneless Chicken Breasts
- 2 Bacon slices
- 8 oz. of Cream Cheese
- ½ cup of Water
- 1 tbsp. of Chives, dried
- 2 tbsp. of Cider vinegar, apple
- 1 ½ tsp. of Garlic powder
- 1 tsp. of pepper flakes, crushed
- 1 ½ tsp. of Onion powder
- 1 tsp. of Dill, dried
- ¼ Black pepper
- ¼ Salt
- ½ cup of Cheddar, shredded

- 1 Scallion, thinly sliced, white and green parts

Directions:

1. Turn on sauté. Once heated add the bacon. Cook until it becomes crispy. Set aside. Cancel sauté.

2. Add the water, cream cheese, chicken, black pepper, salt, dill, pepper flakes, onion powder, garlic powder, chives, and vinegar. Cook for 15 minutes at high pressure. Quick release the pressure.

3. Place the chicken in a plate and shred it. Return into the Instant Pot.

4. Add the cheese and stir.

5. Top with scallion and crispy bacon and serve.

5. Simplified Delicious Turkey Breast

Prep: 5min/**Cook:** 10min/**Total:** 15min
Servings: 2/**Calories:** 251/**Fat:** 1g
Protein: 57g/**Carbs:** 2g

Ingredients:
- 16 oz. of Turkey Breast (2 pieces, fillets)
- 1 cup of Water
- 1 tbsp. of Garlic powder
- 1 tbsp. of Rosemary
- ½ Tsp. of Sage
- 1 tbsp. of Rosemary
- ¼ Tsp. of Black pepper
- ½ tsp. of Salt
- ½ tsp. of Thyme

Directions:
1. Place a rack in the pot.
2. Rub the spices and herbs on the meat and place in the pot, on the rack.

3. To fill 1 cup of water into the pot. Close the lid and set "poultry". Adjust time to 10 minutes.

4. Once done, quick release the pressure and remove the meat.

5. The liquid can be used as a broth for later use.

6. Serve the turkey with veggies you like and enjoy!

6. Turkey Chili

Prep: 15min/**Cook:** 30min/**Total:** 45min
Servings: 8/**Calories:** 270/**Fat:** 12g
Protein: 32g/**Carbs:** 8g

Ingredients:
- 1lb. of ground Turkey
- 1lb. of ground Beef
- 15 oz. of Black Beans
- 15 oz. of fire-roasted tomatoes, diced
- 8 oz. of tomato sauce
- 1 Celery stalk, chopped
- 2 smaller Bay leaves

Spices:
- ½ tsp. of Cayenne
- 1 tsp. of Black pepper
- 1 tsp. of Salt
- 2 tsp. of Ground cumin
- 1 tbsp. of Oregano, dried

- 3 tbsp. of Chili powder

Directions:

1 Turn on sauté. Once hot add the turkey. Cook for 5 minutes and break the meat. Add the beef and repeat.

2. Add all spices, onion, and celery. Cook for a few minutes, and stir.

3. Add tomato sauce, diced tomatoes, and back beans. Pour ¼ cup of water and add the bay leaves, Stir well.

4. Close the lid and cook for 15 minutes at high pressure. Let the pressure release naturally.

5. Uncover, and discard the bay leaves. Stir well. Adjust seasoning if needed.

6. Serve with the toppings you like.

7. Whole Chicken

Prep: 10min/**Cook:** 30min/**Total:** 45min
Servings: 10/**Calories:** 335/**Fat:** 19g
Protein: 38g/**Carbs:** 0

Ingredients:

- 4 lb. (1 whole) Chicken
- 1 tbsp. of Coconut oil
- 1 tsp. of Paprika
- 1 ½ cups of Chicken Broth
- ¼ Tsp. of Black pepper
- 1 tsp. of Thyme, dried
- 2 tbsp. of fresh Lemon juice
- 6 Garlic cloves, peeled
- ½ Tsp. of Salt

Directions:

1. In a bowl combine black pepper, salt, thyme, and paprika. Stir and rub the seasoning outside the whole chicken.

2. Heat the oil in the pot. Add the chicken and brown for 6 minutes with the breast side downward.

3. Flip and add garlic cloves, lemon juice, and broth.

4. Close the lid and cook at high pressure for 25min.

5. Release the pressure naturally.
6. Remove the chicken from the pot and let it rest for 5 min. before carving.
7. Serve and enjoy!

Chapter 7 – Pork Recipes

1. Veggies Pork Tenderloin

Prep: 10min/**Cook:** 20min/**Total:** 30min
Servings: 499/**Calories:** 480/**Fat:** 25g
Protein: 45g/**Carbs:** 7g

Ingredients:
- 1 Pork Tenderloin, Black pepper and roasted garlic
- 4 cups of Broccoli florets, fresh
- 1 cup of Chicken broth
- ½ cup of Red Cabbage, sliced

Lime Sauce:
- 1 tsp. of Water (or more, if needed)
- Black pepper and salt to taste
- Optional: 1 tsp. of Sweetener
- ½ lime, the juice
- 2 tsp. of liquid aminos, or soy sauce

- 2 tbsp. of almond butter or peanut butter

Directions:

1. Prepare the lime sauce. In a bowl, combine the ingredients for the sauce. Stir well and add more water if needed, in order to reach the thickness you like.

2. Now, in the pot, place the trivet.

3. Add the broth.

4. Place the meat on top of the trivet.

5. Close the lid and cook at high pressure for 5 minutes (for medium, 7 minutes).

6. While the meat cooks, boil the broccoli for 5 minutes in a saucepan with 1-inch water.

7. Once the meat is done, let the pressure release naturally.

8. Open and transfer the pot content into a plate.

9. Serve with the veggies and drizzle with the sauce. Enjoy!

2. Juicy Chops

Prep: 10min/**Cook:** 30min /**Total:** 40min
Servings: 6/**Calories:** 280/**Fat:** 10g
Protein: 35g/**Carbs:** 7g

Ingredients:
- 2 lbs. of Pork chops, boneless, sliced
- 14 oz. of Tomatoes, diced
- 1 Jar of Tomato Sauce
- 16 oz. of Green beans, frozen
- 1 tbsp. of Italian seasoning
- 1 tsp. of Garlic salt

Directions:
1. Place the meat in the pot.
2. Add the frozen green beans.
3. Chop the tomatoes and add them in the pot together with the tomato sauce.
4. Sprinkle with seasonings.
5. Close the lid and set to 30 minutes, at high pressure.
6. Let the pressure release naturally. Adjust seasoning if needed.
7. Serve and enjoy!

3. Carnitas

Prep: 10min/**Cook:** 25 min/**Total:** 35min
Servings: 8/**Calories:** 215/**Fat:** 11g
Protein: 21g/**Carbs:** 6g

Ingredients:

- 3 lbs. of Pork butt or pork shoulder, cut into cubes
- 1 onion, diced
- ¾ cup of orange juice, fresh
- 6 Garlic cloves, smashed (peeled)
- ¼ cup of Lime juice, fresh
- 1 tsp. of Chipotle powder
- 2 tsp. of Salt
- 2 tsp. of dried oregano
- 1 tbsp. of Chili powder
- 1 tbsp. of Cumin
- 2 tbsp. of cooking oil or ghee

For serving:

- Lime wedges

- Sliced Jalapenos
- Avocado, cilantro
- Romaine Lettuce

Directions:

1. In a jar, combine the chipotle powder, salt, oregano, chili powder, cumin, lime juice, and orange juice. Mix well.

2. Turn on sauté and add the ghee. Brown the pork. Press Cancel.

3. Add the mixture and add the garlic and onion.

4. Close the lid and cook on high pressure for 30 minutes. Once done, naturally release the pressure.

5. Serve with lettuce wedges and the toppings. Enjoy!

4. Pork Roast

Prep: 10min/**Cook:** 30min /**Total:** 40min
Servings: 12/**Calories:** 282/**Fat:** 20g
Protein: 23g/**Carbs:** 0

Ingredients:
- 4 lb. of Pork Shoulder, cut into 4 equal pieces
- 1 tbsp. of Olive oil
- ¼ cup of Spice blend for pork
- ½ cup of Beef broth

Directions:

1. Rub the meat pieces with the spice and oil.
2. Brown the meat in the instant pot with the sauté mode on.
3. Add the broth and close the lid. Cook 30 minutes at high pressure.
4. Let the pressure release naturally.
5. Serve and enjoy!

5. Cauliflower Pork Bowl

Prep: 10min/**Cook:** 15min/**Total:** 25min
Servings: 4/**Calories:** 330/**Fat:** 27g
Protein: 18g/**Carbs:** 3g

Ingredients:

- 2 cups of Cauliflower, fresh
- 2 tbsp. of Butter
- 2 cups of leftover pork roast
- ¼ cup of Jalapeno slices, pickled
- ¼ cup of Onion, diced
- 2 oz. of softened cream cheese
- 1 cup of Cheddar, shredded
- ¼ cup of Bacon, cooked and crumbled
- ¼ cup of Heavy cream
- 2 tbsp. of Green onion, sliced

Directions:

1. Chop the cauliflower into small pieces. Cook or steam until tender.

2. Turn on sauté mode and once heated, add the butter, jalapeno, and onion. Cook until soft.

3. Add the leftover pork and softened cream cheese. Cook until the cheese is heated.

4. Stop the sauté mode and add the cauliflower, heavy cream and cheddar. Stir quickly.

5. Serve sprinkled with green onions and crumbled bacon.

6. Tomato Chili

Prep: 10min/**Cook:** 30min/**Total:** 40min
Servings: 8/**Calories:** 207/**Fat:** 23g
Protein: 20g/**Carbs:** 5g

Ingredients:
- 1 lb. of ground Pork
- 1 lb. of ground Beef
- 3 chopped Tomatillos
- ½ Onion, chopped
- 1 tsp. of Garlic powder
- 6 oz. of Tomato Paste
- 1 chopped Jalapeno pepper, plus the seeds
- 1 tbsp. of Cumin, grounded
- 1 tbsp. of Chili powder
- ½ tsp. of Salt or to taste
- ¼ to 1 cup of Water

Directions:
1. Brown the ground meat, both pork, and beef in the instant pot on sauté mode.
2. Add the remaining ingredients. Mix well.
3. Close the pot and cook for 30 minutes at high pressure.
4. Let the pressure release naturally.
5. Serve with low or no carb side dishes or as it is, and enjoy!

7. Ribs in 30 minutes

Prep: 5min/**Cook:** 30min/**Total:** 35 min
Servings: 6/**Calories**: 387/**Fat:** 29g
Protein: 27g/**Carbs:** 2g

Ingredients:
- 5 lbs. of Pork ribs, cut into pieces (country style)

Dry Rub:
- 1 ½ tbsp. of Salt
- ½ tsp. of Coriander, grounded
- ½ tsp. of Allspices
- 1 tbsp. of Erythritol
- 1 tsp. of Paprika
- ½ tsp. of Black pepper
- 1 tsp. of Onion powder
- 1 tsp. of Garlic Powder

Sauce:

- ½ tsp. of Onion powder
- ½ tbsp. of Allspices, grounded
- ½ tbsp. of Mustard, grounded
- ¼ tsp. of Liquid smoke
- ½ cup of Ketchup, reduced sugar
- 2 tbsp. of Wine vinegar, red
- 2 tbsp. of Erythritol
- ½ cup of Water
- Optional: ¼ tsp. of Xanthan Gum

Directions:
1. Season the meat with the ingredients for the rub.
2. Place the ribs in the pot.
3. In a bowl, combine the sauce ingredients. Stir well.
4. Pour the mixture in the pot, over the meat
5. Close the pot and cook for 30 minutes at high pressure. Let the pressure release naturally.
6. Transfer the ribs into a plate. Keep them warm.
7. If using, add the Xanthan Gum into the sauce. Turn on sauté and cook until the liquid thickens.
8. Serve and enjoy!

8. Pulled Pork

Prep: 5 min/**Cook:** 30min/**Total:** 35min
Servings: 6/**Calories:** 395/**Fat:** 31g
Protein: 26g/**Carbs:** 0.7g

Ingredients:
- 2 lbs. of Pork shoulder or Pork butt
- ¼ tsp. of Cayenne pepper
- 1 tsp. of dried oregano
- ¼ tsp. of ground Cumin
- 1 tsp. of smoked Paprika
- 1 tsp. of Paprika
- 2 cloves of Garlic
- 1 tsp. of Salt
- ½ tsp. of ground Black pepper
- (Optional) 1/3 tsp. of Cinnamon
- 1/3 cup Broth
- For garnish: 1 tbsp. of chopped green onion

Directions:
1. Cut the meat into 5-6 pieces. Place it in the pot.
2. In a bowl, combine the spices and sprinkle the meat. Coat well.
3. Add the garlic and the broth.
4. Close the pot and cook for 30 minutes at high pressure.
5. Once done, let the pressure release naturally.
6. Transfer the meat into a plate and shred.
7. Serve garnished with green onion and with lettuce leaves or cauliflower.

Chapter 8 – Eggs and Dairy

1. Burrito Bowl

Prep: 10min/**Cook:** 15min/**Total:** 25min
Servings: 4/**Calories:** 613/**Fat:** 50g
Protein: 23g/**Carbs:** 6g

Ingredients:
- 6 Eggs, large
- 3 tbsp. of Butter, melted
- 1 tsp. of Salt
- ¼ tsp. of Black pepper
- ½ lb. of Sausage breakfast, cooked
- ½ cup of Cheddar cheese
- ½ cup of Salsa
- 1 cubed of Avocado
- ½ cup of Sour Cream
- ¼ cup of Green onion, diced

Directions:
1. In a bowl combine the melted butter, eggs, black pepper, and salt.

2. Turn on sauté mode and adjust the heat to less.

3. Add the mixture and cook for 7 minutes; 4 minutes into the cooking, add the cheese and cooked sausage.

4. Divide the eggs among 4 bowls. Top with avocado, sour cream, salsa, and diced green onion. Enjoy!

2. Stuffed Avocado

Prep: 10min/**Cook:** 4min/**Total:** 14min
Servings: 4/**Calories:** 320/**Fat:** 30g
Protein: 12g/**Carbs:** 5g

Ingredients:

- 2 Avocados, ripe and large
- 4 Eggs
- Black pepper and salt to taste
- ½ cup of crumbled Bacon
- ½ cup of Cheddar cheese, shredded
- sliced chives for garnish

Directions:

1. Discard the pits of the avocados and remove some flesh to make a space. Keep the removed flesh to use for another recipe.
2. Place them in a basket for steaming.
3. Pour 1 cup water into the pot and place the basket.
4. Crack each egg in a measuring cup to pour them in the avocado halves.
5. Season with black pepper and salt to taste.
6. Top with cheese and bacon.
7. Close the lid and cook for 4 minutes at high pressure.
8. Quick release the pressure.
9. Transfer the avocados on a plate and garnish with sliced chives.
10. Serve right away and enjoy!

3. Cheddar Bacon Salad

Prep: 10min/**Cook:** 5min/**Total** 15min:
Servings: 6/**Calories:** 290/**Fat:** 20g
Protein: 17.5g/**Carbs:** 4g

Ingredients:
- 4 Eggs, boiled
- 2 tbsp. of Mayo
- 1 tsp. of Mustard, yellow
- 4 Bacon strips, cooked then crumbled
- ¼ cup of Cheddar, grated

Directions:
1. Boil the eggs in the Instant Pot.
2. After they have cooled down, peel and crumble in a bowl.
3. Add the mustard and mayo. Mix to combine.
4. In the instant pot with sauté mode on, fry the bacon until it becomes crispy.
5. After the bacon has cooled down, crumble and add it into the mix. Mix well.
6. Serve!

4. Spicy Egg Avocado

Prep: 10min/**Cook:** 5min/**Total:** 15min
Servings: 6/**Calories:** 315/**Fat:** 28g
Protein: 10g/**Carbs:** 7.4g

Ingredients:
- 8 Eggs, large, boiled in the instant pot.
- 1.2 cup of Mayo
- ½ cup of Salsa
- ½ cup of chopped Celery
- ½ cup of chopped Onion
- 1 Avocado, large
- 2 tbsp. of Lime juice
- Black pepper and salt to taste
- 1/8 tsp. of Cayenne pepper or to taste

Directions:
1. Boil the eggs in the instant pot. Peel and chop them.

2. Discard the seed of the avocado and scoop out the flesh into a bowl. Mash well and add 2 tbsp. of Lime Juice.

3. Add the remaining ingredients. Fold gently.
4. Season with black pepper, salt, and cayenne.
5. Refrigerate before serving. Serve with mango or as desired and enjoy!

5. Fast and Simple Egg Salad

Prep: 5min/**Cook:** 5min/**Total**: 10 min
Servings: 3/**Calories:** 521/**Fat:** 52g
Protein: 23g /**Carbs:** 2g

Ingredients:

- 8 Eggs, large, boiled in the instant pot
- ½ cup of Mayo with coconut oil
- 1 tsp. of Mustard, grounded
- Black pepper and salt to taste

Directions:
1. Boil the eggs in the instant pot. Peel after cooling down, and slice them.
2. Place the eggs in a bowl and add the mustard and mayo. Mix and break the eggs.
3. Season with black pepper and salt to taste.
4. Serve!

6. Egg Bacon Sour Cream Salad

Prep: 5min/**Cook:** 5min/**Total:** 10 min
Servings: 6/**Calories:** 180/**Fat:** 11g
Protein: 16g /**Carbs:** 1g

Ingredients:

- 3 Eggs, large, boiled
- ¼ cup of Mayo
- ¾ cup of diced Celery
- ¼ cup of Sour cream
- ½ tsp. of Chives, dried
- ½ Tsp. of Mustard powder

- 1 tsp. of Parsley, chopped, fresh
- 8 bacon strips, cooked and then crumbled

Directions:
1. Boil the eggs using your instant pot so that you get the best result. Cool them down and peel. Chop the eggs.
2. Cook the bacon and once cooled crumble.
3. Now, in a bowl, combine the ingredients and mix well.
4. Serve with cabbage or lettuce leaf and enjoy!

7. Egg Avocado Wonder

Prep: 5min/**Cook:** 5min/**Total:** 10min
Servings: 6/**Calories:** 162g/**Fat:** 13g
Protein: 8g/**Carbs:** 3g

Ingredients:
- 6 Eggs, boiled
- 2 ripe Avocados, diced
- ¼ cup of Red Onion, minced
- ½ Lemon
- 2 tsp. of Dill, fresh
- ½ Tsp. of Black pepper
- ½ tsp. of Salt

Directions:

1. Boil the eggs in your Instant Pot. Once done, cool them down in an ice bath and peel. Dice and place them in a bowl.

2. In the same bowl add the flesh of the avocados and stir. To make it creamer, stir more.

3. Squeeze ½ Lemon and add black pepper, salt, dill, and onion. Stir to combine.

4. Serve right away!

Chapter 9 – Quick Snacks

1. Cauliflower Hummus

Prep: 10min/**Cook**: 8min/**Total**: 18min
Servings: 8/**Calories**: 140/**Fat**: 12g
Protein: 4g/**Carbs**: 5g

Ingredients:

- 18 oz. of Cauliflower, frozen
- 1 cup of Chicken broth
- ½ tsp. of Sea salt
- 2 tsp. of Cumin, grounded
- ¼ tsp. of Coriander, grounded
- 1 Lemon, the juice
- 2 tsp. of Olive oil

- 3 Garlic cloves pressed
- ½ cup of Tahini

Directions:

1. Add the cauliflower in the pot and add ½ cup of broth. Cook for 8 minutes at high pressure.

2. Quick release the pressure. Drain the excess liquid.

3. In a bowl, add the cauliflower, and add lemon juice, coriander, cumin, garlic, olive oil, salt, and tahini.

4. Blend with immersion blender until creamy.

5. Serve as a spread or a dip, and enjoy!

2. Cauliflower Tots

Prep: 5min/**Cook:** 15min/**Total:** 20min
Servings: 8/**Calories:** 54/**Fat:** 8g
Protein: 2g/**Carbs:** 0.5g

Ingredients:

- 1 ½ lb. of Cauliflower, riced
- ¼ cup of Avocado oil
- 1 Egg, large
- 1 ½ cup of Mozzarella
- 2 Garlic cloves, minced (optional)
- ¾ tsp. of Sea salt

Directions:

1. Turn on sauté mode on the instant pot and stir-fry the riced cauliflower with 2 tbsp. of oil. This will take about 5 minutes.

2. In the meantime, in a bowl, crack the egg and whisk. Add the seas salt, garlic and mozzarella. Mix again.

3. Once the rice is done add it to the egg mixture while hot. Stir well.

4. Form balls from the mixture using a cookie scoop.

5. Wipe the instant pot using a paper towel.

6. Turn on sauté and add 2 tbsp. oil (the remaining), and cook the tots in one layer. Fry for 2 minutes. Flip and cook for 2 more minutes. Transfer to a plate with paper towels in order to drain them.

7. Repeat with the remaining tots.

8. Serve and enjoy!

3. Cauliflower rice

Prep: 5min/**Cook:** 10min/**Total:** 15min
Servings: 4/**Calories:** 35/**Fat:** 0.3g
Protein: 2g/**Carbs:** 3g

Ingredients:
- 1 lb. of Cauliflower florets
- 2 tbsp. of Butter
- Black pepper and salt to taste
- Any optional seasoning

Directions:

1. Wash the florets and make sure that you dry them.

2. Put the florets in a food processor and blend them until they become rice like.

3. Turn on sauté on the instant pot and add butter. Once heated, add the "rice" and season with black pepper and salt. Cook for 5-10 minutes, depending on how you like your cauliflower.

4. Serve and enjoy!

4. Boiled Egg

Prep: 1min/**Cook:** 5min/**Total:** 6min
Servings: 12/**Calories:** 62/**Fat** 4g:
Protein: 5g/**Carbs:** 0

Ingredients:

- 1 cup of Water
- 12 Eggs

Directions:
1. Pour water in the pot. Place a steam rack or an egg rack and place the eggs.
2. Now close the lid and cook at high pressure, 5 minutes.
3. Release the pressure naturally for 5 minutes and then quick release.
4. Place the eggs in an ice bath. Let them sit in the bath for a few minutes.
5. Serve or store no more than 7 days in the fridge.

5. Artichoke Snack

Prep: 3min/**Cook:** 9min/**Total:** 20min
Servings: 4 -6/**Calories:** 250/**Fat:** 12g
Protein: 11g/**Carbs:** 5

Ingredients:

- 2 x ½ lb. artichokes
- 4 garlic cloves, minced
- 2 tbsp. of Butter, unsalted
- ½ Tsp. of Salt
- 1 lemon, the juice

Directions:
1. First, wash the artichokes in cold water. Let them sit for about 5 minutes.
2. In the instant pot, pour 1 cup cold water. Place a rack.
3. Place the artichokes.
4. Close the lid and cook for 9 minutes at high pressure.
5. In the meantime prepare the garlic butter. Turn on medium-low and place a pan on the stove. Melt the butter and add the garlic. Sauté until it becomes golden brown (don't burn it). Set aside and season with salt.
6. Quick release the pressure and transfer the artichokes on a plate.
7. Serve with the garlic butter and enjoy!

6. Steamed Asparagus

Prep: 5min/**Cook:** 1min/**Total:** 6min
Servings: 2/**Calories:** 25/**Fat:** 3g
Protein: 4g/**Carbs:** 1g

Ingredients:

- 8 Asparagus spears, trimmed and washed
- 1 cup of water
- 1 tbsp. of Butter, melted
- Black pepper and salt to taste
- ½ cup of Bacon, cooked and then crumbled

Directions:

1. Place a steamer basket in the pot. Add 1 cup of water.
2. Place the asparagus in the basket.
3. Close the pot and cook at low pressure for 1 minute.
4. Quick release the pressure.
5. Serve drizzled with butter. Sprinkle with bacon and season with black pepper and salt to taste. Enjoy!

7. Spiced Nuts

Prep: 5min/**Cook:** 10min/**Total:** 15min
Servings: 8/**Calories:** 350/**Fat:** 36g
Protein: 4.5g/**Carbs:** 2.4g

Ingredients:
- 4 cups of Pecans
- 4 tbsp. of Rosemary, fresh, chopped
- 2 tsp. of Himalayan salt
- ¼ tsp. of Smoked Paprika
- ¼ tsp. of Onion powder
- ¼ tsp. of Garlic powder
- 2 tsp. of Lemon zest, fresh
- ¼ cup of olive oil
- ¼ tsp. of Cayenne pepper (for heat, optional)

Directions:
1. Turn on sauté mode.
2. In a bowl, mix all ingredients together. Make sure to coat well.
3. Once the instant pot is heated, add the nuts.

4. Cook, stirring constantly for 10 minutes.

5. Once done, sprinkle them with lemon zest and transfer into a baking sheet to cool down.

6. Serve and enjoy!

7. Store leftover in a jar.

10. Keto Desserts

1. Cinnamon Apples

Prep: 5min/**Cook:** 2 min/Total: 7min
Servings: 4-6/**Calories:** 20/**Fat:** 0g
Protein: 0g/**Carbs:** 5g

Ingredients:

- 3 Apples
- 2 tsp. of Cinnamon
- 1 tsp. of Maple syrup

Directions:

1. Core, peel and then slice the apples.

2. Combine the maple syrup, cinnamon, and apples together.

3. Pour ¼ cup of water and coat.

4. Place them in the instant pot. Close the lid and cook for 2 minutes at high pressure. Remove the lid.

5. Serve and enjoy!

2. Strawberry Compote

Prep: 5min/**Cook:** 1min/**Total:** 6min
Servings: 8/**Calories:** 9/**Fat:** 0
Protein: 0/**Carbs:** 2g

Ingredients:

- 1lb of Strawberries, fresh, trimmed
- 4 tbsp. of Orange juice, fresh, blended
- 1 tsp. of Chia seeds
- 1/8 tsp. of Vanilla powder

Directions:

1. Chop the strawberries and place them in the pot together with the vanilla and orange juice. Close the lead and cook at high pressure, 1 minute. Once done, let the pressure release naturally for 15 minutes. Quick release the pressure.

2. Turn on sauté mode and add the chia seeds. Cook for 2 minutes.

3. Let the strawberries cool completely before storing in the fridge. It will thicken once cooled.

4. Serve and make sure it is used in about 10 days.

3. Lime Curd

Prep: 10min/**Cook:** 10min/**Total:** 20min
Servings: 20 oz. (2 tbsp. per serving)/**Calories:** 61g
Fat: 6g/**Protein:** 0.1g/**Carbs:** 0.2g

Ingredients:
- 1 cup of Native
- 2 Eggs, large
- 2 Eggs, the yolks
- 3 oz. of Butter, unsalted, at room temperature

- 2/3 cup of Lime Juice
- 2 tsp. of Lime Zest

Directions:
1. In a bowl, mix the native and butter for 2 minutes.
2. Add the yolks and the eggs. Mix for 1 minute.
3. Add the lime juice. Mix.
4. Pour the mixture in mason jars (half-pint jars) and close with a lid just until it catches; not tightly.
5. Pour 1 ½ cups of water in the pot and place the trivet. Place the jars inside.
6. Close the lid and cook for 10 minutes at high pressure.
7. Let the pressure release naturally.
8. Remove the jars, open them and add the zest. Stir. Again close them lightly.
9. Let them cool before placing them in the fridge. Refrigerate overnight.
10. Serve and enjoy!

4. Coconut Custard

Prep: 5min/**Cook:** 30min/**Total:** 35min
Servings: 4/**Calories:** 174/**Fat:** 15g
Protein: 5g/**Carbs:** 6g

Ingredients:

- 1 cup of Coconut milk, unsweetened
- 3 large eggs
- 1/3 cup of sweetener like Truvia
- 3-4 drops of Pandan extract

Directions:
1. In a bowl, combine the pandan extract, sweetener, milk, and eggs. Mix well.
2. Pour into a bowl that is heatproof. Cover with aluminum foil.
3. Pour water in the pot (2 cups) and place the trivet. Place the bowl.
4. Cook for 30 minutes at high pressure. Let the pressure release naturally.
5. Cool until set, and then serve.

5. Mug Cakes

Prep: 5min/**Cook:** 10min/**Total:** 15min
Servings: 1 mug/**Calories:** 200/**Fat:** 18g
Protein: 6g/**Carbs:** 5g

Ingredients:

The Base
- 1 Egg
- 1/3 cup of Almond Flour
- 1 tbsp. of Maple syrup
- 1/8 tsp. of Salt
- ½ tsp. of Vanilla

Raspberry Cake:
- 1 – ½ tbsp. of Chocolate chips, sugar-free
- ½ cup of Raspberries (frozen or fresh)

Blueberry Cake:
- ½ cup of Blueberries

Directions:

1. Combine the ingredients for the base. Add the raspberry or blueberry ingredients. Combine.

2. Scoop into a mason jar (8 oz.) but don't overfill. (Spray the jar with oil).

3. In the pot pour 1 cup of water and place the trivet.

4. Cover the jar with aluminum foil and place in the pot.

5. Close the pot and cook for 10 minutes at high pressure.

6. When done, quick release of the pressure.

7. Remove the jar and let it cool down.

8. You can serve chilled or warm. Enjoy!

6. Cheesecake

Prep: 10min/**Cook:** 20min /**Total:** 30min
Servings: 6/**Calories:** 190/**Fat:** 18g
Protein: 4g/**Carbs:** 2g

Ingredients:
- 2 tsp. of Lemon Juice
- ¼ cup of Sour Cream
- 2 tsp. of Vanilla extract
- ½ cup of the baking blend, Swerve
- 2 eggs
- 8 oz. of Cream cheese

Topping:
- 2 tsp. of Swerve
- ¼ cup of Sour Cream

Directions:
1. Make sure all ingredients are at room temperature.
2. Turn on Sauté mode and pour 2 cups of water. Place the trivet.
3. In a blender, add the ingredients except for the toppings and eggs. Blend well.
4. Now add the eggs and blend just to mix them, in 20 seconds.
5. Line a springform pan with paper. Pour in the mixture, then cover with foil.
6. Place the pan in the pot. The water should be almost boiling.
7. Close the lid and let it cook for 20 minutes at high pressure. Release the pressure naturally.
8. Mix the swerve and sour cream together.
9. Take the cheesecake out from the pot and top with the mixture.
10. Make sure you cool the cake well because warm or hot is not tasty.
11. Once chilled, take it out from the pan and serve.

7. Peanut Cheesecake

Prep: 5min/**Cook:** 17min/**Total:** 23min
Servings: 8/**Calories:** 190/**Fat:** 16g
Protein: 6g/**Carbs:** 4g

Ingredients:

- 2 Eggs
- 16 oz. of Cream cheese
- 2 tbsp. of Peanut butter, powdered
- 1 tbsp. of Cocoa
- ½ cup of Swerve
- 1 tsp. of Vanilla Extract

Directions:
1. All ingredients must be at room temperature.
2. In a blender, add the eggs and cream cheese. Blend until it becomes smooth, and then add the remaining ingredients and mix just to combine.
3. Now, add the mixture in 4-8 oz. jars. Cover with a lid or foil.
4. Pour 1 cup of water into the pot. Place a trivet.
5. Place the jars in the pot. Cook in batches.
6. Cook for 17 minutes at high pressure. Once done release the pressure naturally.
7. Chill the peanut cheesecake overnight or a few hours.
8. Top with heavy cream, whipped and drizzle peanut butter. Serve and enjoy!

8. Peanut Bites

Prep: 10min/**Cook:** 15min/**Total:** 25min
Servings: 8/**Calories:** 250/Fat: 23g
Protein: 5g/**Carbs:** 4g

Ingredients:
- 1 cup of Erythritol, powdered
- 16 oz. of softened Cream Cheese
- ¼ cup of Sour cream
- ½ cup of Peanut Flour
- 2 Eggs
- 2 tsp. of Vanilla extract

- 1 tbsp. of Coconut oil
- ¼ cup of Chocolate chips, low-carb

Directions:

1. In a bowl, combine erythritol and cream cheese. Beat until smooth. Add the vanilla, sour cream and peanut flour. Fold gently. Fold the eggs until combined.

2. Pour the batter into 4-inch pans or cupcake molds, and cover them with foil.

3. Add 2 cups of water into the pot. Place a rack.

4. Lower the pan into the pot. Close the lid and cook for 15 minutes at high pressure. Once done let the pressure release naturally.

5. Let the cups cool and place them in the fridge.

6. In a bowl, add the coconut oil and chocolate chips. Microwave until melted and smooth. Drizzle over the cups. Chill.

7. Serve and enjoy!

Conclusion

With all 80 recipes in this book, you won't ever get bored cooking. This is especially because you will be using your instant pot. You have recipes to add in your meal plan that are tasty and easy, and they will never throw you off ketosis. Well, this is the most important part. Just make sure you combine the right meals to get the right carbs intake.

What I like about these recipes is that most of the ingredients are things you already have at home. What you will need to get are just a few ingredients and start cooking. No, you will be letting the instant pot cook for you. It is time to forget all about getting smelly when cooking. You and your home will be free of smelly odor and still, when the meal is ready, it will be flavorful and delicious.

There is a reason why keto has become so popular. It is because it really helps reach your goal, whether weight goal or health. Most importantly, it is easy to follow and you are allowed to have desserts as long as it can be fitted to your daily carbs intake. Moreover, you can eat cheese, bacon, and meat without restrictions. High fat intake is important because this will keep you satisfied and get rid of the sugar cravings. On the other hand, protein needs to be taken in moderate levels. Too much protein can also destroy ketosis.

Few other things to remember are to always have fresh ingredients and buy the best products if possible, especially for organic and lean meats. This will not only help you with keto, but it is overall healthy.

Keto can be enjoyed with the whole family, and can be easily followed because you won't be even aware that you are on a diet with all the delicious food on the menu. Is your family skeptic about your new diet, and your new lifestyle? Well, it is time to change their mind and cook them a keto meal with your instant pot. They will immediately understand why keto is your choice and why you choose to cook with your instant pot.

You can get a lot of help in enriching your diet and replenishing your body with essential nutrients through the use of specially developed keto-complexes.

Any diet is a restriction on the supply of certain nutrients. Keto diet in this regard is no exception. You almost wholly exclude carbohydrates from your diet, so it is highly desirable for you to use certain supplements and vitamins so that the body tolerates stress more efficiently. You can do without them, but if you want to be sure that you do not harm your health, then it is better to use at least the basic ones.

As promised, I am sharing with you the products that I use myself for the best stay in Keto.

Basket №1 - the main set for a beginner https://iherb.co/LDCdqojS

this includes a multivitamin complex explicitly adapted for men or women; calcium and magnesium in one bottle, potassium, omega 3, vitamin D.

Basket №2 - for advanced users https://iherb.co/FLFtwEaw
Here we also have a vitamin complex explicitly adapted for men or women, calcium citrate, magnesium and potassium quotes.

Products that I buy here, I share my best practices with you https://iherb.co/D4uMBGcy

Made in the USA
Middletown, DE
09 May 2020